THE SIBERIAN CAT

ALICE E. WRIGHT

Published by Picky Press

The Siberian Cat

Copyright © 2020 Alice E. Wright

Print ISBN: 9781643949994

EBook ISBN: 9781643949987

Library of Congress Control Number: 2021909706

www.kendersiberiancats.com

Published by Picky Press, an imprint of Tovim Press, LLC.
Phoenix, Arizona, USA.

PickyPress.com

TABLE OF CONTENTS

My many thanks to those who helped and inspired me. As always, any mistakes or omissions remain mine.

CHAPTER 1

THE SIBERIAN CAT:

AN INTRODUCTION

Most Siberian breeders and authors claim a great antiquity to this breed. Yet cat breeding is a relatively new phenomenon only dating back less than 200 years. While animals have been selectively bred for thousands of years it was generally for more obvious purposes such as horses for heavy pulling, or dogs for hunting, guarding or flock tending. The art and science of keeping cats, specifically "purebred" cats, has only come around since primarily the nineteenth century Victorians. And since cats were not bred to pull heavy loads, tend flocks, or guard homes, they have been selectively bred for aesthetics, or in other words, their looks. But

1

that doesn't mean cats weren't an integral part of human society for a very long time.

Many would contend that cats have been kept for thousands of years, as mousers to keep one's home and barn free of rodents. Man's earliest attempts at domestication can be traced as far back as 10,000 years ago as humans learned to harvest grains, which were subject to those rodent infestations. But these cats were not contained as dogs and horses were. Instead, they were allowed to freely roam and breed without human interference until very recently. They learned to hunt in the grain and fields thus developing, what might be called a symbiotic relationship with man.

Defining a breed within any species can be brought down to its most basic level. A "breed" is considered any group of animals, (in this case cats, and more specifically *Siberian Cats*), that have unique characteristics, which when interbred, will be passed down in successive generations. Simplified, when "cat A" is bred to "cat B", all the kittens have the same phenotype as the common parentage. Phenotypes are the observable characteristics; those that we can see.

For a longhaired cat, this means that both parents must carry the longhair gene. Each parent gives a single copy of the gene to the kitten and two copies of the gene are needed; the longhair gene being recessive.

In the case of the Siberian, it is referred to as a "natural breed". Natural breeds are those types of animals that have developed over the course of time without man-made influence on them. Yet geographic restrictions and naturally occurring mutations seem to be its primary cause of creation.

The Siberian hails from one of the most unforgiving, harsh, and extreme climates known to man today, as well as one of the widest territories for a landrace. For this breed to survive, it took many special adaptations that are still very evident today.

The oily outer coat helps protect the cat so that nothing penetrates to the skin to cause the cat to become cold, wet, or injured. The tufts on the ears for protection from ice and wind. The tufts on the pads of the feet to better help walking across snow, sometimes many feet deep. The eyes being deep-set and "hooded" which offer protection from winds and snow. The "fat belly" or sometimes referred to as a "famine belly"

that is evident even in young kittens, and might remind you of a bear being able to store its fat for winter. The claws being able to retract further into the pads of the cat most likely to prevent breaking into the snow and ice. And of course, its claim to fame being the hypoallergenic qualities, which may very well be an adaptation to limit its scent, and therefore be able to hunt more effectively and stay hidden from larger predatory animals such as wolves more easily.

New evidence published in 2007 from research that was funded by the National Institutes of Health, leads some to believe the Siberian an ancient breed, perhaps the "first" breed. The researchers concluded that, "So, domestication for sure, took place in the Middle East where those cats live today." (Stephen J. O'Brien of the National Cancer Institute).

Another more current study dated July 2020 presents what is the earliest evidence for a domestic cat (*Felis catus*) from a well preserved skeleton with extensive osteological pathologies dating to 775–940 cal CE from the early medieval city of Dzhankent, Kazakhstan.

Furtuosity's Nikita

Nigel

TICA Regional Winner Quad Grand Champion
Kender's Golden Boy

Kender's Big Kahuna

CHAPTER 2

FACTUAL ORIGINS OF THE SIBERIAN CAT

The genetic and historical aspects of the Siberian appear to be very old indeed. *The Book of the Cat* lays the claim that "long hair appears to have originated as a gene mutation in southern Russia, spreading to the cat populations of Turkey and Iran to show up in the Angora and Persian breeds".

Theories abound as to the origin of the Siberian, but many of these same theories are applied to other breeds, such as the Persian and Angora. One school of thought even implies that the Persian is, in fact, not really "Persian" at all. These cats may be mistakenly associated with Persia due to the cats first having been seen from ships hailing from the Middle East.

An article published in June 2007 by the Associated Press, quotes Stephen J O'Brien of the National Cancer Institute as saying, "So, domestication, for sure, took place in the Middle East where those cats live today".

Mitochondrial DNA was studied in 979 cats including our domestic cat, wild cats from Europe, Asia, and Africa. What was found, was that the DNA was virtually identical. Earliest evidence of domestication seems to be from Cyprus approximately 9,500 years ago. Large feline predators have also been depicted in the early first millennium CE in Persia, as seen on rhytons dating to the Parthian period (The Metropolitan Museum of Art, New York, Cat.: 1979.447) and much later in metal objects from the twelfth and thirteenth centuries CE.

The recorded history of the Persian can be traced back to the early 1520s, but its origin can never be fully proven. One theory is that the Persians stemmed from cats known as Angoras, which had originated from Turkey. This would then support the 2020 findings of an intentional domestic cat burial discovered in Kazakhstan, dating back to 950 CE, by A.F. Haruda and team. The supposition is that these cats were then permitted to be crossed with other longhairs from Persia, Afghanistan, Burma, China, and further parts of Russia, following what is today known as the Silk Road, which existed from around 207 BCE–220 CE.

Cats from this known heritage were brought into Europe via Italy and France in the late 1600s. In a book published in 1876, long haired cats were referred to as Asiatic cats, an area that would have encompassed southern Russia, which would tend to substantiate the claim of the Siberian breed being the "original" long hair.

Historically, the first cats were thought to have been brought to the area of the Volga about the 6th century B.C. From there, they gradually spread to the north up to the Baltic sea region and further East. It is known that the domestic cat (*Felis catus*) originated from the African cat (*Felis silvestris lybica*), and that the European wild cat (*Felis silvestris silvestris*) did not play a significant role in its development or the development of domesticated cat breeds; although it could have interbred with the domestic cats brought into Europe by the Romans. Following this theory, Norwegian Forest Cats would then have the same basic origins as the Siberian, being descendants of the African cats once brought into Europe, Central and Northern Asia through Asia Minor, following the established ancient merchant route, the Silk Road. But here the similarities would end, and each unique breed would diverge to meet geographical demands and needs.

One doesn't find mention of cats in Russian annuals or other historic documents prior to the 14th century, when in the criminal code, the fine for killing a cat was set at the same level as for killing an ox. But the nearer to Asia Minor, the earlier we can meet aboriginal cats in the territory of Russia.

The wars of Ivan the Terrible ended with annexation of Astrakhan in 1556 (lower Volga) and Kazan (mid-Volga). As part of the spoils of war, the czar included several large shaggy cats he took back to Moscow, keeping them in the palace to catch mice.

And while we don't know what those cats looked like, they are very likely the earliest ancestors of the modern Siberian.

It is interesting to note that there seems to have been a shift in the value of the domestic cat sometime between the 1500s and the 1700s. There is a book entitled *West of the Revolution: An Uncommon History of 1776* that discusses a group of the Aleut people during this time, who caught a ship traveling to Yakutsk in Russia, and further into Kyakhta following the highly profitable fur trade at the time. Yakutsk is located about 450 kilometers south of the Arctic Circle, and Kyakhta is located on the Kyakhta River near the Mongolia–Russia border. In this traveling, Russians eagerly traded China for silks, teas, cottons and rare herbs. What this has to potentially do with Siberian Cats, is that the Russians in return traded many millions (or so it is quoted) of fur pelts including sable, fox, and domesticated cat. One can only presume the old law of protection was either forgotten or struck down perhaps as the population grew and needs changed.

In the year 1745, Empress Elizaveta Petrovna, daughter of Peter The Great, signed a decree ordering that cats were to be found in the city of Kazan and brought to her court in Moscow:

Better cats, the largest ones, able to catch mice and accompanied by a person who will look after their health.

Empress Elizaveta's reign was to be only 20 years before she died. Her reign was not a glowing one in regards to attaining wealth or power for Russia, but she is widely regarded as the founder of the educational and cultural revival. She brought to the country the giant baroque masterpieces of the (then unfinished) Winter Palace, which later came to include the Hermitage Museum, among other national treasures. We of course will regard her as the beginning of a great heritage for the Siberian Cat.

Upon Empress Elizaveta's death was a brief transition of power to Peter III Feodorovich, who only ruled for a short six months. His wife Catherine the Great succeeding them both as the longest ruling female leader by Russian standards. And remember by this time, there was already a large number of cats at the Winter Palace.

In 1793, the well-known and documented German zoologist and botanist, Peter Simon Pallas observed what he documented as a colorpoint cat near Mokshan town on the Volga river. He had been contracted by the Empress Catherine the Great, and was cataloging the plants and animals of Russia, traveling in southern Russia from 1792-1793. His work proving that the colorpoint gene, (to be discussed later in Chapter 4), is clearly already in the Russian countryside.

The Book of the Cat by Francis Simpson published in 1903, makes several references to a Russian Longhair. Another early mention, most likely of our Siberian breed, is in Harrison Weir's book *Our Cats and All About Them* originally published in 1889, in England. Weir was a well-known British artist and cat lover who studied cats for almost half a century, giving us the first standards for all (at the time) recognized breeds and colors. These were published in his book where he describes Siberians in his chapter entitled "Russian Cats". Weir describes this breed by writing:

It differed from the Angora and the Persian in many respects. It was larger in the body with shorter legs.

The mane or frill was very large, long and dense, and more of a wooly texture, with course hairs among it; the colour was of dark tabby, though the markings were not a decided black, nor clear and distinct; the ground colour was wanting, in that depth and richness possessed by the Persian, having a somewhat dull appearance.

The eyes were large and prominent... the ears large by comparison, with small tufts, full of long wooly hair, the limbs stout and short, the tail being very dissimilar, as it was short, very woolly, and thickly covered with hair the same length from the base to the tip...

These Russian cats were only one of three recognized longhaired breeds shown at the first-ever cat show in London, England in July 1871 held at the Crystal Palace. The other two longhaired breeds Weir recognized were the Persians and Angoras. There has been some debate whether or not a Siberian was actually at this show, or if Weir's writings were pure conjecture. Considering Weir, himself, produced this show, he was in the best position to record the details and relate his experiences of it.

He made clear distinctions between the qualities of the three breeds, including coat and tail lengths between the Persians, Russians, and Angoras. In the same chapter entitled "Russian Cats", Weir recalls how he only "bred but one kitten from the Russian" and that "I have seen several Russian cats..." These comments leave no room for debate. He did own such a cat and had personal experience with them.

The above engraving was originally published in 1813, in the book entitled *Rural Sports*, and reprinted in Weir's book. Note the similarities to a modern-day Siberian Cat both in features and coat.

We also find mention of a cat by the breed name of "Siberian Cat" in a 1883 Show Catalog printing that was held in Boston. This is an entry into the Catalogue of the Grand American Cat Show, held at the

Horticultural Hall in Boston, on Monday October 15th 1883. "Entry No. 163" for that day of the competition, was listed as a Siberian Cat named "Snowball", a solid white cat (presumably male), owned by Alexander Anderson. I believe this may be the earliest documented "Siberian" cat to be exhibited at a Cat Show in the United States. Potentially proving the link between the forested breeds of cat for genetic purposes.

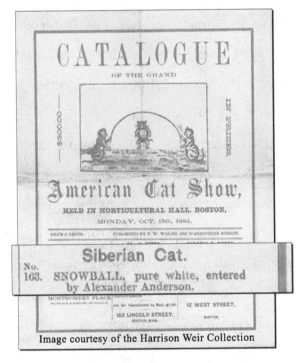

Image courtesy of the Harrison Weir Collection

By comparison to the Maine Coon cat, considered America's oldest longhaired natural cat, was also exhibited at a few shows in this early stage, including an 1878 Boston cat show, the 1883 Boston show, and most likely an 1880 show. The history of Maine Coon cats and their early participating in cat shows was extensively documented by Mrs. E. R. Pearce, who herself was an owner of a Maine Coon cat named "Captain-Jinks of the Horse-Marines". In fact, this black and white Maine Coon is the first documented in literature on the breed, (not in show catalogs).

In 1926, Dr Jumaud's book *Les Races des Chats* (The Breeds of Cats), which seems to be largely based on works by Professor Cornevin of Lyons, described what was called a "Tobolsk cat":

> *It is larger than our common cat, and somewhat resembles the Carthusian in shape. The head is large, with big eyes, short nose, and small erect ears. Coat: as is fitting for an animal of a cold country, the Tobolsk cat has long fur, longer than that of the Chartreuse cat. Its texture is woolly, and in colour, uniformly reddish.*

Sadly, with the rise of the Communist Party in 1917, it would seem that the Siberian would pass largely into the shadows. Pet ownership was actively discouraged, and in some cases, officially restricted.

And so for decades, no official documentation appears on the Siberian. Even world wars were to play an interesting and potentially critical part of both the breed's virtual extinction and resurrection.

It's been well established that the Winter Palace Hermitage in St. Petersburg is home to a huge collection of art. Perhaps less well known until recently, is that there has been a veritable army of cats guarding the treasures from rodents even after all these years, and this tradition continues even today.

Even the uprising of 1917 by the Bolsheviks did not dislodge the cats and their caretakers. While the October Revolution drove Tsar Nicholas II from the Palace along with their dogs, the cats were essentially ignored and remained in place.

WWII, and the Siege of Stalingrad

This unyielding assault, occurred from late 1941, and didn't end until January 1944. It was during this epic battle that the Germans managed to completely seal off the city. The brutal combat, by both sides, completely destroyed the city's infrastructure. Getting food into the city was an impossibility, and as a result, the people turned to any means necessary to survive .Even small animals such as cats, dogs, and rats became food for the desperate citizens.

And still the death count from exposure, German artillery, and starvation was enormous. The terrible fighting, living in rubble, and having to survive on these small animals led to this being referred to as *Das Rattenkrieg*, or "The Rat War". The end result of this long engagement with significance to the Siberian

Cat's story, was a nearly complete annihilation of the feline population. And as is nature, with no cats as predators, the rodent population soon expanded to exponential numbers, destroying what little food was available and wreaking havoc on the human population.

Once the siege lifted, several creditable sources indicate that the Soviet government gathered thousands of cats, shipping them by train into the city to help control the rodents. One survivor's diary is quoted in the *Pravda.Ru*, saying that a train full of smoke-colored cats from the Yaroslavl area, came into Leningrad in April of 1944.

The Yaroslavl area is approximately 175 miles north of Moscow on the right bank of the Volga River. These cats were then released; some say simply into the streets to fend for themselves; while others claim they were parceled out and exchanged for bread rations. In either case, these cats were hard working rodent killers who managed to survive through to modern times, yet retaining their basic temperament traits we see today in their obvious descendants whom we call simply "the Siberian".

After 3 years, the cats returned to their previous job of rodent killers and have remained there ever since. These first cats were brought from Yaroslavl in 1943 when the blockade was first breached, marking a turning point in the battle for the city. Blue smoke cats from Yaroslavl were considered good rat catchers and were in great demand, even though one kitten could cost ten times the price of a loaf of bread.

A fantastic and rare find of black and white photographs was recently discovered and acquired by Kender Siberians.

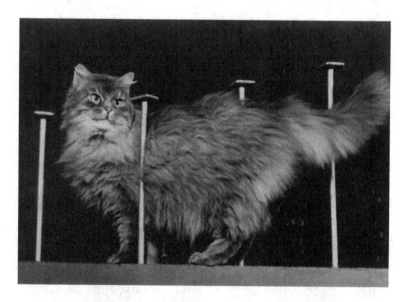

First, we see a wonderful promotional piece for a family circus, printed in the late 50s or early 60s.

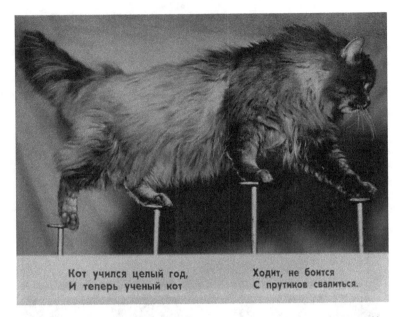

Кот учился целый год,
И теперь ученый кот

Ходит, не боится
С прутиков свалиться.

The big beautiful blue longhaired cat is easily archetypal of a Siberian Cat. The caption below it is translated to: "The cat has been trained the whole year, and now being a learned cat he can walk on the sticks and twigs without fear" (*translation by T Vasiliv with our thanks and gratitude).

Next is a semi-series of 2 photographs. First, we see a group of four people and their pet cats, who were taken aboard the SS Lakeland Victory, after being released by the Chinese communists, who held them as prisoners for more than a year.

This picture is labeled as follows: "Pictured from left to right, is Mrs. Angus Ward holding 'Jeep' a cat born in Vladivostok, Siberia. Consul Angus Ward holds 'Sai-Khan' born in China. Vice Consul William Stockes holds 'Saki', born in Munden, and Miss J Norwicka, the family maid, holds 'Ranger' born in Vladivostok." This picture is dated December 24, 1949!

This wonderful candid is of General Consul Angus Ward back on US soil in a family home in Allegan, Michigan. What makes this picture so significant, is it is labeled, "Jeep, a Siberian cat which traveled".

This picture is dated January 1, 1950! Proving without

a shadow of a doubt that 1) this cat was considered a Siberian Cat, and 2) this cat was now on US soil, 40 years prior to the first "official" importation of the breed! Also, as cats were rarely kept inside and were permitted free roam, it is exceptionally likely that this cat mated with the local domestic population and could (and should) be considered a potential contributor into our own domestic Maine Coon gene pool.

In the 1980s, with Gorbachev's political reforms firmly in place, cat clubs were formed, records were established, and shows were held in the former USSR.

The history of the cat fancy in Russia is controversial, as is much of Russian history. According to Irina Sadovnika, the first Soviet cat exhibition/show was held in Riga, Latvia in 1986 by the club "Felimurs".

This was closely followed by a much larger show held in Moscow in 1987 by the club "Fauna". It was from this show that the magazine *Cat Fancy* (Oct 1988) featured an article on the show and the clubs. It was reported to draw a crowd of 80,000 spectators!

Due to the political climate, and food and housing shortages, ownership had been discouraged. But apparently the breeders were not! Beginning in 1986, official organizations began record keeping throughout the Soviet Union, which at that time encompassed 11 time zones! Each was operating as its own entity, registering their own member's cats, and issuing pedigrees and critiques as competition grew between the clubs. In these early years, the cat clubs sought to more closely align themselves with FIFe, the international European registry.

The judges for these first shows came mainly from Czechoslovakia. Again we refer to Irina Sadovnika as she wrote, "In the catalogues of the first shows we find, apart from imported Persians, lots of Maine Coons, Norwegians, Balinese, and Turkish Angoras... All these novice pets were found in the streets and taken from friends whose non-pedigree cat had kittens. Semi-longhaired cats provided the widest opportunities for fantasy. Every owner looked at their pet and tried to find a feature in common with the beautiful pictures of pedigreed cats printed in books".

Their disappointment after the show in "Kotofei" was great. Out of a group of several dozen, the judges accepted only one cat. The judges explained that the cats entered were too massive; even cobby, with heads that were too broad, and their legs and tails were not long enough. The only common feature was the waterproof semi-longhair coat.

And so, it was decided on the advice of these judges by the participating exhibitors and owners, to create a new breed based on the aboriginal Russian cat population.

The members of the first cat club "Kotofei" in St. Petersburg (formerly called Leningrad), began looking at their cats more selectively, trying to establish common features. Possibly the most well-known name in Siberian pedigrees today is "Roman", who was used as the example for the first written standard in 1987, by the then president of Kotofei, Olga Mironova. In February of 1988, Siberians were judged for the first time using this standard.

In 1989, several clubs joined together to form a new independent registration body called the "Soviet Felinological Federation". One of its first actions was to certify the new breed calling it the Siberian Cat (as certificate #1) and its colorpoint variant otherwise known as the "Neva Masquerade" (as certificate #2).

Here is where much debate and argument has ensued. Within the breeders of Siberians in the US and elsewhere, there seems to be primarily two schools of thought.

One group firmly believes that color pointed cats could not survive in the "wilds" of the Russian land; are not "native" to the land, having been introduced through outside means of Thailand or China, and as such should not be included as a part of the Siberian breed.

The second group contends that, as one of the founding cats "Max", who was a seal lynx (tabby) point, contributed a significant gene variation into the modern-day Siberian, and as such it cannot be ignored at best, or selectively bred out at worst. But who is correct? So, we must return to the documentation of the time.

All through the late 1980s, cat shows were being held in Russia, St. Petersburg, and the surrounding regions. The cats that had previously failed in attempting to gain a foundation status for currently known and widely accepted breeds (being the Maine

31

Coon, Balinese, and Turkish Angora), now were doing very well using the newly written Siberian standard.

These loved street cats had now found a place and a value in the show world. By the end of 1990, this "new" breed had attracted the attention of many worldwide exhibitors and fanciers.

By 1991 The Siberian Cat was on the international scene, since Kotofei and other Russian clubs had joined with WCF (World Cat Fancy) who itself had been founded in Brazil in 1989 by the initiative of its first President Mrs. Anneliese Hackmann. The WCF accepts the Siberian in semi-longhaired breed category and recognizes almost all colors and patterns including the colorpoint, or Neva Masquerade. Also in 1991, the head of the breeding committee for Kotofei would travel to Rostock, Germany to discuss the provisional Siberian standard. And of course, the first three pedigreed Siberians made their way into the US, thanks to the dedicated work of Ms. Elizabeth Terrell.

It is important to note the distinction of the word "pedigreed" here. Because we "know" that in 1883 in

Boston there was a cat on US soil called a Siberian; but where that cat went from there, or what happened to him, we do not know. And we know that in 1949/50, two longhaired cats of Russian birth were brought over into the US as pets.

A "purebred" Siberian, imported from Russia, is given a Certificate of Birth called a "Metrika" with the proper seal and signatures of the authorities for that particular club/registry. Even in the early 1990s, the Russians warned that not all cats labeled as "Siberians" were in fact pedigreed. Just as many people refer to any longhair as a Persian or Angora, so too did the Russians have a tendency to call almost all longhaired or semi-longhaired cats a "Siberian".

In December of 1991 the USSR dissolved into The Commonwealth of Independent States. Today the problem of confusing all longhairs with Siberians has generally been alleviated. The collapse of the Soviet Union heralded in a new way of life. Widespread access to the internet has opened up communication; translations are easier to obtain, and are more reliable.

THE SIBERIAN CAT

Even the former president of the USSR, Mikhail Gorbachev was photographed with his pet cat for *Time Magazine*. This picture ran in the March 9, 1992 edition. It is a widely held opinion that the cat is a Siberian.

Although the Communists discouraged pet ownership, it seems the Russian people still embraced their lovely early Siberian type cats as both friends and family.

The following are photographs of the everyday life and love of cats in Russia . . .

CFA Grand Premier Regional Winner Kender's Lady Sherade
and future CFA Grand Champion Kender's Toujours Pur

CHAPTER 3

THE SIBERIAN CAT'S MOVE
INTO THE UNITED STATES

In 1987, the first cat show was held in Moscow with a recorded attendance of 80,000 people. A detailed article with many photos appeared in the October 1988 edition of the magazine *Cat Fancy*. This article was written by Nikolai Nepomnyashchi who was at the time, vice chairman of the Cat Owners Association of the Russian club Fauna. The article included 10 photographs, including one of a Siberian Cat. Specific mention was made at that time about this breed being native to the Soviet Union and putting a comprehensive breeding program in the planning stages. This article ended by asking to establish ties with American cat clubs and breeders.

Elizabeth Terrell of Starpoint Cattery who was a Himalayan breeder, was intrigued by this article. The editor of the Atlantic Himalayan Club's newsletter *Cat Tracks* ran a single paragraph in the winter 88-89 edition claiming there were no Himalayan Persians (color pointed) in the Soviet Union, and asked if anyone would be willing to donate one or two to help establish that breed.

Letters were written, most being hand-carried. And eventually after much planning, the first-ever three Himalayans were sent to the Russians and the first three Siberian Cats arrived in the US in June of 1990. These cats came from the registering club "Kotofei", a word meaning "cat friends". Although most of the old Soviet Union's purebreds were lost for all time during the many wars, and pet ownership was openly discouraged due to housing and food shortages, people began breeding and forming clubs to record registrations, ownership, and matings as previously discussed around 1986.

These three cats, which arrived in Louisiana, were the basis for many of the catteries here in the

US. The names of these now famous "first three" cats are Kaliostro Vasenjkovich of Starpoint, Ofelia Romanovna of Starpoint, and Naina Romanovna of Starpoint. And so it began. Ms. Terrell soon imported twelve additional cats in May of 1991.

Alice Wright (then Schreiber) of Kender cattery had been raising and showing Siamese for a while, and Audrey Oliver of Furtuosity cattery had primarily Maine Coons. They got quite a surprise when a visiting Russian professor and her translator came back for a second visit. They brought with them their first Siberian who arrived in November of 1992. A young golden ticked tabby female by the name of Karoline's Aldan Abakan who was later to have the cattery name of "Furtuosity" added to her registration and be co-owned by both catteries.

This female was later to become the US's first Champion of record through the American Association of Cat Enthusiasts (AACE). This cat is also significant to the Siberian breeding history, as she was from a different region, and of a different pedigree and background than the original Starpoint lines, thus adding a whole new dimension to the

Siberian gene pool available for the decades to follow, coming into the US.

She is the foundation queen for both Kender and Furtuosity Siberian Catteries. Karoline only produced a single litter of three kittens. A red classic male that was kept by Furtuosity and later transferred to Kender for breeding, Furtuosity Illya Veetovich. The second kitten, also a red classic tabby male, was neutered as a kitten and kept by Kender Cattery. This boy, Furtuosity's Serge Veetovich, was shown extensively in every major organization in the US, used in demonstrations in schools, exhibitions for the public, and to introduce the breed. "Serge" lived a long and full life finally passing at the age of 15. Having been born in 1994, he displayed the breed's beautiful characteristics of not only type, but temperament.

Serge earned multiple championships, grand championships, as well as regional and national awards during his career. The third kitten was a red tabby and white boy that was sold to a lady in New York, Furtuosity's Ivan Veetovich.

The next two kittens for Kender arrived in the spring of 1993, a brown-ticked tabby female Zinka Jacklineovna, and a red mackerel tabby male Nestor Jakovich. These kittens were shown briefly, and their photos have been lucky enough to be reproduced numerous times in many publications worldwide, thanks to the professional services of Chanan Feline Photography.

Starpoint's Veet Caliostrovich of Furtuosity

In 1994, Furtuosity cattery bought one of the offspring of the originally imported boy from the Starpoint cattery, Kaliostro Vasenjkovich, a brown classic tabby and white. This boy, Starpoint's Veet Kaliostrovich of Furtuosity and later of Kender, added a great deal of type and substance to both breeding programs. Also in 1994, several other catteries in the US got their start with the Siberian. Most were coming from the Starpoint lines, such as Croshka in Georgia and Windrifter in Minnesota; but some like Kravchenko imported their first Siberians independently, adding to the gene pool in the US.

An event of importance in 1997 was the first import into the US of the color-pointed Siberian. Willowbrook cattery, out of California brought in these first two colorpoints. Color pointed cats were deliberately left out of the original breed standard by Elizabeth Terrell. She was told that they were considered a separate breed rather than a simple color variation. Even though, called "Nevsky Masquerade" in its native land, it is not considered two breeds. Here in the US, in almost all associations, colorpoints are considered a simple color variation, and shown as a single breed.

In 1998, the first color pointed kittens were born to Willowbrook cattery.

In 1999, three Siberians were sent to Japan from the US cattery Kravchenko, thus establishing the breed on the island nation of Japan.

Since that time, many other breeders have built upon these foundations, both by bringing new lines from the country of origin and other countries where the

Siberian has been an established breed for many years, such as West Germany. There are now several clubs available to hobby breeders and fanciers alike.

Most are affiliated with a particular registering body such as CFA or TICA. Others such as TAIGA, are independent clubs. Every cat association/registry in the US now accepts the Siberian for championship competition, thanks to the long hours, many dedicated people, and monies invested in the promotion and exhibition of these beautiful and unique cats.

Furtuosity's Nikita Illyavitch

As mentioned previously, not all cats that are longhaired and come from Russia are pedigreed Siberians. There should be some mention of an early attempt at almost the same time as Mrs. Terrell, by a man out of New Jersey to "be the first" to import Siberians. He had contacted the same breeder that Mrs. Terrell had been working with, and was emphatic about being in a rush and wanting to buy six cats. Although turned down by the Russian breeder, he claimed to be working with, and purchased a cat from a West German breeder. At that time, it is reported he told her "since they all came from strays..." "there would not be pedigrees anyway". And while the ultimate kernel of that statement is true, it does not mean they are to be considered Siberians. This could readily be where many people have been scammed and gotten a cat or kitten without a proper pedigree or documentation. It was believed that in the US previously, he had Norwegian Forest Cats.

It was later discovered and reported by Mrs. Terrell in 1993 that this same man had left the US after some legal and financial problems, had supposedly given up his cats, and purportedly married the then President of the FAUNA cat club in Russia. This same cat club had been rejected by FIFe two previous times and had changed names to the "All Union Cat Club" in a conjoined effort with other Russian clubs to gain admittance. CFA, at that time was affiliated with the FAUNA club but did not want to affect ties with FIFe.

CFA (Cat Fanciers Association) is the largest cat association in the world today. Organized in 1906, their first two shows were held that same year in

Buffalo and Detroit respectively. In 1909, CFA published the first-ever stud book in a book format.

Since that time, CFA has become a leader in the fancy, and the standard that most breeders strive to achieve. However, in the world of the Siberian, CFA was the last hold-out for championship status in the US. All other registries had previously accepted the Siberian for championship over the course of time. Finally in 2006, the Siberian Cat was recognized for full championship status, including the much-debated colorpoints.

One of the first Siberians to achieve the title of Champion (and possibly the first) was a black smoke and white male, Kender's Deutsch Schwarzes Gold. This cat was bred by Kender Cattery and owned by TranSiberie Cattery out of Oregon in 2006.

This same cat then went on to produce the first CFA Grand Champion, and the first Grand Champion Premier. Produced by Siberkot Cattery, they are CFA Grand Champion Siberkot Rocky Mountain and CFA Grand Champion Premier Transsiberie's Lunar Attack. Rocky was also awarded CFA's Best Siberian of the year award for the 2006-2007 show season.

CFA Judge Bob Zenda with a young CFA Grand Champion Kender's Don't Call Me Nymphadora

Currently, the Siberian Cat ranks #15 in CFA's registration numbers, showing the consistency and popularity of the breed.

In TICA (The International Cat Association), Siberians came onto the scene a bit earlier. They were accepted for championship by 1996, and the colorpoint added into the standard in 1997.

Early Supreme Grand Champions and Regional winners were SGC Troika Zahar Ahlmazovich, and SGC Trezkuchiy Sibirskiy Moroz Mur.

In the 2000-2001 show season, SGC Trezkuchiy Sibirskiy Moroz Mur "Irdie" owned by the late Judge Judy Chapetta, is first Siberian Cat of the Year in TICA. Such a huge accomplishment from a breed that literally was unknown by US exhibitors 10 years prior.

Siberians continue to make huge inroads in TICA. In the 2012-2013 show season, another lovely Siberian was Cat Of The Year, this time it was IW SGC Mittelmeijer Roskoshniy Kot Mur, and who also happens to be related to TICA's 1st Siberian COTY – Irdie. It is exciting to see the Siberian so well received, and rewarded over the years in the competition show rings. But what might be even more exciting is to see the Siberian actually have his own movie! A really cute movie was released in 2016 entitled *Nine Lives*. And the star, while billed as its human actors, really is the Siberian Cat – Jean! (Jean, a.k.a. CFA Regional Winner, Breed Winner, and Grand Champion Jean Sineglaziy Angel of Sineglazka.)

And while Jean did have a couple of stunt doubles as well as a mechanical stand-in, who else in the cat fancy can say they have a whole movie they are a part of? Pretty impressive!

Did you know Siberians can also have odd eyes occasionally?

CFA Grand Champion Sineglazka's Modern Love of Kender

CHAPTER 4

COLORPOINTS:

SIBERIANS OR NOT?

Among today's breeders, there is a distinct split: the battle lines, if you will. You have one faction of the fancy who consider themselves traditionalists. These breeders claim that the colorpoint could not have been a part of the original gene pool, and that a color pointed cat would not survive because he would not be able to blend in and camouflage himself. Some even go so far as to claim that with blue eyes, the reflection of the sun off of the consistent snows would render the cat blind.

Many base their information on supposition and theory. Others base it on the fact that the first cats brought into the US did not display the color pointed pattern nor produce it. And in fact, what little written history is to be found on the Siberian, there is no indication or hint that a color pointed cat was part of the original gene pool in historical aspects.

However, one item to remind the reader from the previous chapter of Siberian history is that the famous scientist Pallas did in fact claim a cat of pointed color to be found in Russia. But if one is to look at the actual drawing done at the time, the reader can readily and without any stretch of the imagination see that the cat described is in fact *not* a Siberian at all, but a Siamese (Thai Cat). The drawing is included below.

Seal point certainly, round of head, but also smooth

and short of coat as well. We can only speculate what that cat was doing on the Volga in 1793. But remember that this was a very important and well-established trade route of the day. So perhaps, many such animals made their way, blurring the lines. And no cat ever looked at another and said, "No thanks to sex. You're not my type!"

Next, you have those that see nothing wrong with having the colorpoints as part of the breed and thus the gene pool. And their arguments are generally quite simple– If the Russians recognize them, then why shouldn't we? While not much of an argument, it certainly is a valid one.

Two of the founding sires within this breed's earliest standards were Mars, a blue lynx point and white; and Max, a seal lynx point, both of whom contributed immensely to the gene pool. And as such, contributed to the establishment of the breed and continuation of type from the very start. At the time of early breed recognition efforts in the US and Europe, no genetic analysis of actual original specimens was possible. Testing had not come anywhere near as far as it has today. A very long mitigating set of circumstances that must be considered is that we have virtually no written history of the Siberian before the 1980s, with only a few notable exceptions.

Russia, and its current Common Wealth of States is even today in a time of flux, as to where and how they fit in the international scene. Prior to today's age, you had a communist country that encompassed literally a dozen time zones, while suppressing (or attempting to suppress) most of its population for generations; and prior to that for hundreds of years you had a feudal style of government with a czar and ruling family or cast.

What is very creditable, are the known journal entries from the time of WWII's Siege of Stalingrad survivors, detailing cats being brought in from all around the country by train. And while no direct government record was kept, it was accepted as fact and documented by the people. Siamese (Thai cats) have a known history of being popular in Russia since around the early 1960s, and were reputedly imported to help in regards to political relations with the Indochina countries. These cats were the classical short-haired color pointed, round-headed cats we see even today. Main ports of entry were St. Petersburg and Vladivostok, which easily explains why the colorpoint gene is abundant in these cities, but rare and even absent in most of the rest of Russia's indigenous cat populations.

The colorpoint gene is a recessive trait meaning each parent must carry one copy of the gene, for it to be expressed. Even if two "traditional" colored cats, carry this recessive gene, both can produce pointed kittens when bred together. And with current levels of genetic testing, a breeder can easily and inexpensively test for those cats who do or do not carry this gene, as their tastes and beliefs follow.

All through the late 1980s, cat shows were being held in Russia, St Petersburg and the surrounding regions. The cats that had previously failed in attempting to gain a foundation status for currently known and widely accepted breeds such as the Maine Coon, Balinese, and Turkish Angora were now doing very well using the newly-written Siberian standard. These loved street cats had now found a place and a value in the show world. By the end of the 1990s, this "new" breed had attracted the attention of many worldwide exhibitors, fanciers, and hobbyists.

Yet the debate still rages. There is a wide chasm that separates Siberian breeders. The vast majority fall onto one side or the other. But ultimately it will be each person's decision.

Pictured below are some lovely colorpoint examples of the breed.

(Courtesy of Prekrasne Siberians)

Colorpoint Kittens (Courtesy of Croshka Siberians)

(Both photos Courtesy of Prekrasne Siberians)

CFA judge enjoying and evaluating a lovely Siberian entry

CHAPTER 5

SIBERIAN STANDARD OF

PERFECTION

ll animals that compete in "beauty" contests are judged by a standard of perfection. Conformation shows are judged with a point scale and physical description. This gives the judge something to compare both to and against.

Each point scale is based upon 100 points assumed for the perfect animal. Each animal is judged against this point scale, with points being appropriately deducted for each fault, as seen and interpreted by the judge.

Following are the point scales within the standards of perfection for both the Cat Fanciers Association (CFA) and The International Cat Association (TICA). The full standards, including physical descriptions and corresponding color descriptions can be found at their respective websites. This is an overview only.

Let us put the point scales together, and see how they compare:

	CFA	TICA
Head	45	40
Body	40	35
Coat/Color	15	15
Other	--	10

These points are pretty similar in all aspects, so you would think judging a Siberian and those being shown in both associations would also be very similar. Both say the head shape is a modified wedge. Both say the ears are medium-large, rounded, and tilt forward on the head. Both call for the neck to be rounded and well-muscled. In fact, the wording is very similar throughout most of the written portion of both standards.

Let us interpret the written portion of the standard and break it down, making it easier to understand. The basic shape of the Siberian is a series of soft circles. Note the phrase "rounded" is used many times in the descriptive portion of the standard. Also, please take note that "rounded" is distinctly different from "round", which the Siberian is most decidedly not.

Let's start from the top– or the head, and work our way down. The head is described as a "modified wedge with rounded contours". "A what", you ask? Think of it this way– A wedge is, simply put, a triangular shape like a piece of pie. It can be a skinny wedge such as the Siamese and Oriental. It can be a moderate wedge such as the Norwegian Forest Cat and Abyssinian. Or it can be a very large wedge such as the British Shorthair or Scottish Fold.

Now in relation to the Siberian, a modified wedge is a medium piece of pie with the corner edges modified to be "rounded" off. There's that word again.

A round head would be that of a Persian or Exotic. Again, a round head would most definitely be undesirable. But "rounded" is correct, and what a breeder should be trying to obtain.

Looking at the head from the top what you should see is a trapezoid with the edges rounded off. With this example of a trapezoid, you can clearly imagine the wedge shape as described in the breeds standard.

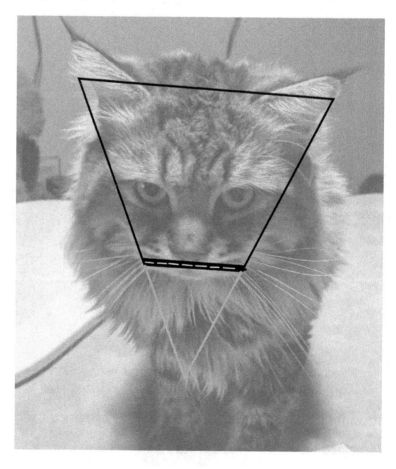

So, the modified wedge described in the various standards morphs into a trapezoid, with the ear placement at the furthest outside edges; rounding the contour, while the muzzle is the smaller end of the trapezoid; again, lending softness to otherwise straight lines.

The ears are medium-large, rounded and tilt slightly forward. The forward tilt gives the cat an alert and intelligent expression. The size of medium-large indicates that the ears sit well onto the head, without being the dominating or eye-catching feature. And

"rounded" indicates that the tip of the ear should be in harmony with the rest of the cat, and not sharp, not tall, and not pointed.

Ear furnishings are the fur growing from the inside of the ear and showing to the outside of the ear. These should be present and full in an adult cat and can give an illusion of a taller ear. The ears should be set as much on the sides of the head as on the top.

Think about that wedge again. In the area where the two top points are rounded, is where the ears should sit. With a moderate degree of back skull, you will get a correct breadth of 1½ ears width apart.

The eyes should be large and almost round. The outer corner angled up and slightly toward the base of the ear. Think of a walnut. This would be the ideal shape.

Some lines show a tendency to have a hooded, or more feral look.

Eye Shape

Provided the eye's basic shape is correct, this is not a fault, but some breeders do not care for it.

The distance should be 1 or slightly more eyes' width apart in the front of the head. Not to the sides.

The muzzle is short, full and well rounded.

The chin is well rounded but in alignment with the nose, neither protruding nor undershot. Both would be considered faults.

The profile of a Siberian is distinctive. When seen from the side, the space from the eye set to the beginning of the muzzle should be concave, allowing for a distinct break. The top of the head between the ears is relatively flat, giving it two defining planes.

The neck is sturdy, thickly muscled in the mature cat and rounded. One might think of a boxer's well-muscled neck when describing the Siberian.

The body is medium in length, well-muscled and strong. The back will be arched slightly higher than the shoulders, with a firm barrel-shaped belly.

The best visual for this is to think of a pear– yes the fruit, on its side. The larger end would be the rump of the Siberian while the narrowed end is where the neck and shoulders join. The body blends into the legs which can only be described as medium, with the hind legs slightly longer than the front. Substantial boning is a must.

Often seen in all Siberians of any age is a primordial pouch. A belly pouch of fat stored behind the belly between the back legs. Many cats have this, but Siberians exhibit this trait most often.

The feet are large and well-rounded with toe tufts even in very young kittens.

The tail is medium in length and tapers ever so slightly to a blunt tip. The overall length is ideally slightly shorter than, but never longer than, the length of the body.

The coat, color, and texture can vary from pattern to pattern, color to color, and even the time of year. Siberians like all Forested breeds of cats carry a triple coat. This is described in detail in another chapter.

Eye color is not linked specifically to any certain coat color in the Siberian, so you may get three red mackerel tabbies that all have differing eye colors, yet all three are correct. The only correlation is a cat with two blue eyes must either be pointed or white.

Kender's Quidditch Captain

Cats that do not have the above qualities, while still being a pedigreed Siberian, can definitely fall into the category of being a pet. A Siberian that displays a narrowed muzzle or an incorrect coat, tall narrow ears or almond shaped eyes, will not make a successful show cat, but is still a sweet and loving pet!

CFA Judge Vicki Nye examining a Siberian entry

CHAPTER 6

TEMPERAMENT AND
YOUR SIBERIAN

The Siberian temperament can vary widely, and depend on a number of factors. Most Siberians are lap buddies, devoted companions, and mischievous. They are strong and agile, easily able to jump from the ground to the top of your refrigerator or even plant shelves. Most Siberians tend to like playing in running water such as from faucets. Some are even quite adept at

opening doors, playing fetch, or sitting up "like a squirrel". And if you happen to have a fish tank, most Siberians consider this something akin to a live action movie.

Many do not like strangers as they tend to be one-person or one-family cats. Russians repute them to be protective of their families and reserved towards strangers. Personal experience has taught me that they are viciously protective of their kittens from would-be dangers, such as dogs. But in all, the Siberian is a tender, sweet, and affectionate kitty very much in tune with their families.

What a difference from the first Siberians exhibited in shows in Russia in the late 1980s. It is widely reported that stewards bandaged their wrists but couldn't avoid being scratched or bitten. And with a show hall full of visitors, the cats were carried up in the air, so they wouldn't endanger the public. Even owners suffered their wrath with bites and scratches.

It took the foundation Siberians a lot of time to acclimate to this new world of shows and exhibitions. Their keen intelligence and curiosity that so helped them to survive as a feral or street cat was not exactly endearing in a show hall. Yet within an extremely small span of years, the Siberian has become a seasoned softie, allowing strangers to play with and examine him without complaint. Many registries have gone so far as to include the phrase "must be non-challenging" in the description of temperament for the Siberian breed.

But as with most things in life, a Siberian will only give to you what you are willing to give to him. If you work long hours and offer little socialization, it is all too easy for a kitten to slip back into a more self-protective mode of the feral type of behavior.

I have always highly recommended early, and lots of socialization for all kittens. Handle, pet, and play with your kitten on a more than daily basis. Make them as much a part of your daily routine as coffee!

Get your Siberian acclimated to traveling within the confines of a crate in a safe manner so that when a trip to the veterinarian or an emergency arises, kitty is comfortable and feels secure.

Their voice tends to be more of a soft chirp or mew, unlike some other breeds that can peel the paint from the walls. Siberians have an almost uncanny ability to converse with you and be able to convey their message. If you are paying attention, there isn't a thing they cannot convey.

If you are buying a kitten, a lot of these factors are in your hands. How you handle your kitten's education and socialization is up to you. Ideally, your breeder will have laid the foundation, but you must provide the continuing education. Your kitten should be friendly and outgoing towards you and possibly your family. Introduce him slowly to other pets and children in a safe and secure way, so as to build the kitten's confidence while ensuring his safety. This can take days or weeks, depending on the circumstances and each individual kitten's personality.

If you are getting an adult cat, you may have a lot of work to do or very little. Confident cats tend to more readily accept new situations, while shy or fearful cats need more time, patience and reassurance.

Even though the breeder may have had a dog, yours will sound and smell different. Children always react individually. Other cats in your home have developed a comfort zone and hierarchy that now will need to be challenged and re-established. So you can reasonably expect a couple of challenges and even down right fights.

Socialization is a must for this breed. Taking a weekly drive, safely from the confines of a crate can be a large benefit.

If you intend to show this animal, or even just go for routine vet visits, this can immensely lessen the stress and trauma if your cat is used to riding in a car in his carrier.

Some stores still stock the old-fashioned cardboard carriers, and we do not recommend these. They are not secure. Your kitty can easily chew out, push out, or simply weigh enough to break through the bottom of this type of container. A crate such as those with plastic sides and a metal door front are what we use and recommend and never, under any circumstances allow a cat to ride loose in your vehicle.

Some Siberians, with gentle patience and understanding, have been taught to walk on a leash. Others have been known to play fetch. Siberians are involved in many areas of pet therapy and rehabilitation in the medical field, while some have been photographed for advertising. And one well-known Siberian has even been the star of a movie!

The Siberian's temperament is flexible, and they readily learn new skills and behaviors. This intelligence cannot be ignored. Left to their own devices they will find ways to entertain themselves. It's your choice. Do you want to spend time with your Siberian, or let your kitty's natural innate intelligence run amok?

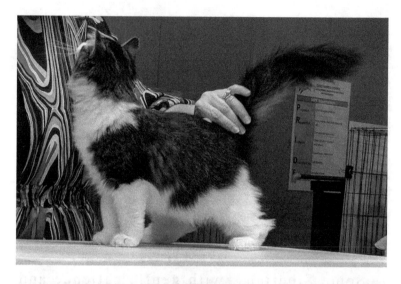

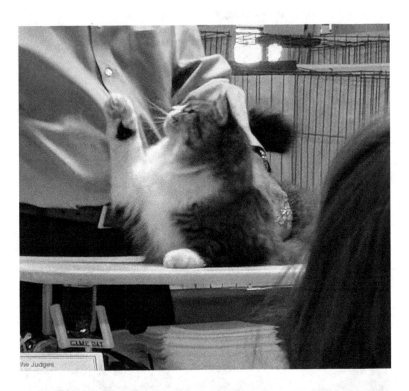

CHAPTER 7

BASIC COAT CARE AND
NUTRITION

All animals need daily interaction to be truly happy and healthy. The Siberian is no exception. With that in mind, daily grooming should begin early with your kitten. This special one-on-one time will not only enhance the already positive temperament traits of this breed, but also secure the bond between you and your cat.

Basic Coat Care

Daily grooming is also an easy way to assess your kitty's overall health, allowing early detection of health changes; which, in some cases, can be lifesaving. A daily combing ritual can be established for even the busiest of schedules.

The main grooming tool is a metal greyhound-style comb, with both wide (called "coarse') and narrow (often called "fine") teeth. A small cushioned pin brush may also be used.

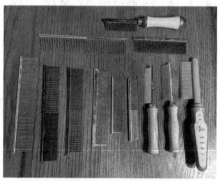

When following this type of routine, it is rare for a Siberian to mat or become overly tangled. Little knots and tangles can be easily combed out using care. The pin brush should be used for general brushing, and to help stimulate the flow of natural oils throughout the coat.

Males naturally carry a heavier, longer coat than females. Altered animals (spayed and neutered) will generally have a heavier coat with less "molting" than intact cats. These are some additional factors to take into consideration when purchasing your Siberian. Molting occurs typically two or three times a year with minimal shedding in-between times in a healthy non-stressed pet. During these times of molting, daily combing is a must, or enormous mats can occur which might require a professional groomer's help.

The mature adult Siberian carries a beautiful full, triple coat. The under coat or "down" hairs are  rather short and lay close to the skin. These hairs act as a warm blanket, insulating the cat from the coldest of weather, and help to keep the cat clean. The second layer is heavy and full, giving the Siberian a larger-than-life appearance, and may add an extra layer of protection from ice or snow. The outer guard hairs are the longest on the Siberian and often appear oily or slick. This is a waterproofing effect much like a duck's feathers. The Siberians that you may see at a cat show will have had a bath to remove this layer of oil to present a "clean" appearance to the judges. However, for the pet cat kept in the home, the removal of the oils is not needed. In fact, regular baths are not generally recommended unless being exhibited or an accident occurs, so long as regular combing and brushing is taking place.

And remember, this is a semi-longhaired breed. "Flowing", as applied to Siberians, does not mean long or "Persian-like". Both of these should be faults in judging.

When choosing your Siberian, the level of grooming will depend on the role this cat will play. If you intend to exhibit your cat, proper grooming is a must. Bathing should be done well in advance of a show and on a regular schedule. Bathing a day or two prior to the show gives the coat time to re-acquire its natural luster, but not the oily sheen that judges will penalize you for. Ideally, the breeder will be able to help you through the first bath, entry into the show, and the show itself. Kitten baths are less time consuming, but more care should be given to ensuring that it's an enjoyable experience. Bathing on a regular basis for a show cat is a must. In contrast, a family pet will not need this, and might not ever need to be bathed.

If you need to bathe your Siberian, either for a show or because of an accident, remember that when bathing your cat, use a shampoo that is safe for them. Most shampoos that are safe for dogs are *not* safe for cats. Be sure to read the label. Your kitten's breeder should be able to steer you in the right direction with suggestions and ideas. Always be sure to thoroughly rinse the coat, as leaving shampoo on the coat will give it a tacky look and heavy feel. Most breeders recommend that after a good rinse, you do a second rinse, both with water, and then even a third, but using a mixture of ½ cup vinegar to 1 qt water. This will help ensure all remaining soap is washed away. Then a final rinse to remove the vinegar smell is typically in order. Bathing for a show is time consuming, but the results can be spectacular.

Once the bath is done, it is on to drying. First, use a good towel to soak up as much of the excess water as possible. Blot with the towel as opposed to rubbing. After this, allow the cat some personal time to de-stress from the bath, letting him run around for a few minutes and shake himself off. However, be sure to keep him contained to a small area such as a bathroom so he doesn't hide under a couch or bed. This will also give you time to count your fingers and toes– just kidding!

If you are not bathing for a show, then you may just want to leave the cat to self-dry, using the time-tested technique of licking itself dry. However, if you are interested in a more "polished" look such as for a show, then a modern handheld ionic blow dryer should be sufficient. If possible, a model with a stand is particularly helpful as it frees both hands. While it may take a while for your cat to accept the noise of a blow dryer, with time and patience, they will accept this as just another thing to endure from us strange humans.

Blow drying your kitten has a few simple rules. First, never use the dryer in the face of a cat. This is, (in cat speak), considered the height of rude, and in kittens can be mistaken for a correction. Second, never use a dryer on high heat. This is extremely dangerous, and can cause burns and the overheating of your cat. And third–patience, patience, patience. Comb slowly and carefully. Talk to your Siberian and reassure him you are not going to torture him forever.

Following these guidelines and being consistent with your Siberian will only help further the bond you two are already developing.

Basic Nutrition

Cats, by their very nature and physical design, are obligate carnivores. This is different from canines which are omnivorous. Many in the canine family such as coyotes, are scavengers who subsist on a wide variety of foodstuffs. But not your kitty, nor any feline– large or small.

Structure alone tells the story of a predator with sharp pointed canine teeth for puncturing, grabbing and holding prey, and a mouth full of molars that do not have occlusal tables [horizontal surfaces] used for shearing and tearing. Even a cat's tongue has coarse barbs to help her separate her dinner from its bone.

To help facilitate its hunting abilities, all cats come with a set of natural instincts to hunt prey, catch it, and kill it. Whether we throw a ball, play with a feather on a pole, or get her to jump after the red laser dot, we are allowing our kitties to express their natural instincts; albeit in a socially acceptable way. This gives us joy to watch, but also gives your kitty mental enrichment and satisfaction she just can't get any other way.

So what does the term obligate carnivore mean? Obligate carnivores are a specialized class of carnivore that solely evolved to eat flesh. They have simpler and shorter digestive tracts than omnivores and herbivores.

This streamlined digestive tract is not designed to handle the cell walls of plants. They have eyes on the front of their heads pointing forward to help facilitate hunting. They have strong, wide-opening jaws that do not move side to side (which is what herbivores have). They have very sharp pointed teeth that do not line up, to hold, rip and tear their meals, not chew. Cats also lack amylase, an enzyme specifically designed to break down plant cells while chewing. Cats even meet their blood sugar requirements by breaking down the protein in the meat they eat, as opposed to getting it from carbohydrates. Simply put, your cat must eat meat to survive. As obligate carnivores living in our homes, it is entirely dependent on us to meet the nutritional needs of our kitties.

All protein is made up from different amino acids and your kitty can only naturally synthesize twelve of these. The rest of these must come from their diet. The eleven amino acids you must supply for kitty to not only survive but thrive, are arginine, threonine, tryptophan, valine, lysine, isoleucine, leucine, methionine, histidine, phenylalanine, and taurine.

The protein in animal tissue has a complete amino acid profile. Plant-based diets don't contain the correct building blocks for optimal health for our feline friends. Long term, this can lead to all types of health problems. This is why all commercial pet foods must have nutritional supplementation.

This leads to the discussion of dehydration in cats which is much more common than most people believe.

Commercial dry pelletized diets do not offer your kitty the moisture they would naturally acquire by eating fresh raw foods.

Domestic cats originated in the arid areas of the Middle East, Egypt, and North Africa. As a result, most cats are less inclined to actively drink from pools or bowls of water. They would naturally get the vast majority of their moisture needs met by eating raw meat.

By feeding dry kibble, we are forcing our pets into an unnatural state of chronic dehydration. Cats, unlike dogs, are not efficient at consuming water from outside sources. Have you ever watched a cat drink? They are lousy drinkers. They often splash and flick it around but their jaws just are not designed to take in large enough quantities of water. By comparison dogs use their tongues like spoons and do a pretty good job of shoveling. Prey species, such as horses and cows can suck large volumes of water very effectively.

When fed a diet of commercial kibble combined with ineffectual drinking, this can lead to chronic dehydration. Dehydration puts stress on the kidneys and can lead to cystitis, and even kidney disease in the long term. You can help change that by having multiple water vessels available, including bowls, fountains, and even the occasional running tap. Giving foods that are fresh and moist can help minimize this as well.

A Pet Expo in Hong Kong highlighting the many different
cat breeds including this exhibit of the Siberian Cat

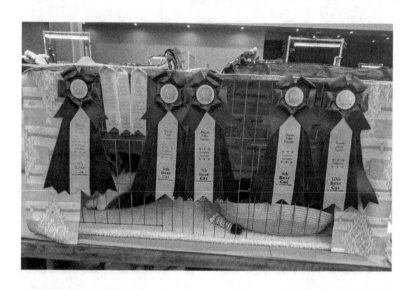

CHAPTER 8

ARE SIBERIANS REALLY HYPOALLERGENIC?

I s the Siberian the answer to your cat allergies? Are they hypoallergenic like you've heard? Is any animal actually hypoallergenic?

Many breeders promote the Siberian as the answer, and you can find many websites that make this claim. However, it is important to review some basic facts before believing the hype.

First, the definition of "hypoallergenic", (according to https://www.sciencedaily.com/terms/hypoallergenic.htm.) is: *Hypoallergenic is the characteristic of provoking fewer allergic reactions in allergy sufferers.*
Hypoallergenic does not mean non-allergenic, just fewer reactions. This term was first used in cosmetics in

the 1950s and there is no governmental or scientific oversight regulating such claims. While no animal can be guaranteed to be lower allergen, this term is freely used and believed within much of the Siberian community.

Allergic reactions begin in your immune system. When an otherwise harmless substance such as dust, mold, or Fel d 1 is encountered by a person who is allergic to that substance, the immune system over reacts by producing antibodies that "attack" the allergen. The most typical signs and symptoms are wheezing, itching, runny nose, watery or itchy eyes. And allergies can both grow and diminish over time. As always check with your doctor for any specific information or assistance.

Black smoke kitten

In 1999, a report out of Cornell University presented evidence that the specific allergen, called Fel d 1 (*Felis domesticus* allergen 1) is the causative agent in approximately 85% of allergic reactions in people.

Fel d 1 is a glycoprotein found in the sebaceous glands of all cats' hair roots and in their sublingual salivary glands. It is also found in the urine of male cats, which would account for why males are more allergenic than females. Previously, it was assumed that only the saliva and/or dried skin of the cat was the offending culprit.

During grooming, the Fel d 1 is distributed along the body and coat of the cat. When this dries and flakes off, it becomes aerosolized. The allergy-causing agent is then free to float about the environment. This "dander" contains the dried presence of Fel d 1. The dander is extremely lightweight being only about 2.5 microns in size. At this size, it can easily stay airborne for hours, and regular air filters are incapable of trapping it. Only certified filters with a capture level of less than 2.5 microns would be able to eliminate such allergens effectively from your home.

Younger cats and kittens, just like children, have less dead and dry skin; Fel d 1 levels can change, and both lessen or grow over time in individual animals, depending on overall health, time of year, and home care. Stress can also cause a sudden surge in allergen levels.

Studies have shown that in any animal, be it pedigreed Siberian or street moggie, intact males have significantly higher levels of this Fel d 1 in their systems than surgically sterilized animals. And animals sterilized early prior to the onset of puberty have the lowest of potential levels. So why do so many breeders tout this breed as being hypoallergenic or non-allergenic? Obviously, this is a great selling point for their kittens, but to-date, no scientific study has been conducted.

An individual submitted samples to Indoor

Biotechnologies in late 1999. The results were interesting to say the least. Only 4 cats were included in this original testing process, a mixed-breed altered male of unknown ancestry, a pedigreed Siberian altered male, a mixed-breed spayed female of Abyssinian descent, and finally a pedigreed Siberian altered female.

Mixed Breed Neutered Male	62813 mcg/g
Siberian Neutered Male	2001 mcg/g
Abyssinian Mix Spayed Female	364 mcg/g
Siberian Spayed Female	205 mcg/g

These results would seem to support the theory that people who might be allergic to "regular" cats could in fact be able to tolerate a spayed or neutered Siberian as a pet. Thousands of people who own Siberians do so because they feel their allergies don't bother them or are at such an acceptable level that cat ownership is no longer a hardship or health issue. However, as to the claim of non-allergenic, you can see for yourself this is simply not the case. These cats can and do still produce measurable levels of the Fel d 1 protein. Many breeders test their cats and kittens while passing those costs onto the consumers. These breeders only use those animals in their programs that have lowered amounts of Fel d 1.

Some cats show as little at 0.5 mcg/g of the allergen. However, this could be a misleading, since we know that Fel d 1 levels can change throughout the seasons and a cat's life and circumstances.

Pet ownership confers numerous health benefits, including positive influences on blood pressure and cardiovascular health. Pets also improve mental health by alleviating loneliness, depression and reducing anxiety.

Many owners consider their cats to be part of the family. For these reasons, allergists' guideline-based recommendations to remove the cat from the home are often met with resistance. Common sense should always be the rule of thumb when any health issues are at stake.

Children, Asthma, and Cats

A 2001 report from the National Institute of Health says that parents shouldn't worry or be too quick to believe that their kitty is the cause of their children's asthma. In fact, studies have shown that cat exposure is different. Thomas A. Platt-Mills, MD and his colleagues at the University of Virginia's Asthma and Allergic Diseases Center conducted a study involving 224 children aged 12 to 14 years. They tested the children for asthma as well as the amount of cat allergen in each child's home. The researchers discovered that children in a low-to-moderate level of exposure did seem to have allergic type reactions. However, those with high amounts of exposure not only reduced the IgE antibodies but also the likelihood of asthma.

IgE antibodies are produced when a person's body responds in a negative way. The high levels of cat allergen, prompted the children's bodies to produce IgG and Ig4 instead. Dr. Platt-Mills was quoted as saying, "This result alters the advice we give patients." However, he does still warn that those with a positive skin reaction test should not risk exposure. (Lancet, March 10, 2001).

So once again, common sense and what works for you and your family is what must prevail when deciding to purchase any cat or kitten.

Many breeders today offer to send fur samples to potential owners, or to use one of your shirts or towels and rub it on their cats and return it to you. Some also offer in-person allergy test visits. All can be good gauges in a minimal way. It is certainly not a final say.

Kittens do not develop hormonal growth until after 4-months of age, so their Fel d 1 levels are naturally lower than an adult cat's would be. And early desexed cats will have a lower level than whole breeding cats, or those who are desexed later in life.

While it is impossible to completely eliminate allergens from your home, there are some steps you can take to mitigate their effects on you and visitors:

- Use a cat litter that does not cause you allergies.

- Place an ionizer within a few feet of the litter box.

- Use HEPA filters for vacuuming.

- Regularly mop hard floors.

- Regularly change your home air filters.

🐾 Clean screens and doors.

🐾 Hard surface flooring instead of carpet (carpet and rugs trap allergens).

🐾 Wash linens every 7-10 days.

🐾 Wipe down your kitty with a wet wash cloth every few days.

🐾 Do NOT allow your cat to sleep in your bed.

🐾 Keep your cat out of the bedroom and establish a "cat free zone".

🐾 Litter scooping should be done by a non-allergic household member or wear a face mask if everyone has allergies.

🐾 Take oral antihistamines.

🐾 Feed a high quality, species-appropriate diet.

🐾 Brush and groom your cat regularly.

🐾 Keep your cat's skin and coat healthy.

This list is not inclusive and you can find many other ways as well to be able to live with a Siberian Cat. As always, consult with your doctor.

An interesting study was published by Purina® in

2019. This study strongly suggests that feeding an avian immunoglobulin equivalent, which are concentrated in chicken egg yolks, will reduce the overall accumulated Fel d 1 levels even in adult cats. Large quantities of these antibodies accumulate in chicken eggs, and can be used to deliver antigen-specific IgY in food. Cats in the study showed a median decrease of 50% of the glycoprotein Fel d 1 and some showed as much as an 86% decrease.

This would seem to lead to the logical conclusion that feeding, as part of a balanced raw diet, an inclusion of raw whole egg on a semi-regular basis would also yield the result of lowering the offending glycoprotein. It would also make sense to look potentially for a breeder who feeds raw as they would, by supposition, tend to have naturally lower levels in their cats as well.

Another concept, or preconception that gets passed around the social media networks of nonsense, is that certain colors of Siberians, or cats in general, are more likely to cause allergic reactions or less likely. This is utter nonsense. No color is any more or less likely to cause allergies. Somehow this very common question or belief crops up frequently. Is this color more or less hypoallergenic? Is that color better or worse for allergies?

The DNA in your cells is made up of many millions of base pairs of nucleotides, which are teeny tiny little molecules that lock together.

When an animal's body needs to make something, like a muscle fiber or an enzyme to digest something for example, the DNA is the recipe it uses to make that protein. A tiny machine called tRNA zips along the DNA strand and grabs these amino acids and lumps them together in the order that the DNA tells them to. The end result is a protein, which the body then uses to do one of a million things with.

If the string of DNA has one or more letter changes (a *mutation*) in it, the protein that the tRNA makes will be different than normal. So *mutations* cause *protein changes*.

One of the things all bodies do all of the time is make *melanin*. That's the color protein. Melanin has a very complex synthesis cycle, and if any of the proteins that go into melanin production are changed, the melanin changes too.

One very common mutation, or change to the melanin protein, is called "temperature-sensitive oculocutaneous albinism". The DNA that makes tyrosinase, (one of the enzymes critical to melanin production), has a very, very small mutation in it. The mutated tyrosinase from that DNA breaks down when it gets above about 30°C/90°F. As a result, the animal can't produce melanin wherever it is over 90°F, but it *can* produce melanin when it's under 90°F.

The result is what we call "color pointed" or "Neva" in Siberian Cats, where the cooler body parts make color and the warmer body parts do not. Now what does this explanation of color have to do with how allergenic my Siberian is? Quite simply– nothing, not one darn thing!

The gene for Fel d 1, the protein that causes the most cat allergies, is on a completely different area and even a completely different chromosome than the tyrosinase gene. The two have *nothing* to do with each other.

Color does not determine allergenicity. It also doesn't determine whether a Siberian is purebred or not, which is another argument you'll get from people who don't like pointed cats, or don't like silver cats, or whatever the color *du jour* is. Color is the result of tiny changes in genes; it does not drag along with it any concept of "pure" and it definitely doesn't drag along with it any allergen production.

Kender's Tiger Lilly

CFA Grand Premier Regional Winner Kender's
Diamond Jim of CrystalStar

CHAPTER 9

BUYING YOUR SIBERIAN CAT OR KITTEN

Once you have fallen in love with the Siberian as a breed and decided you can't live without one, your search begins. You need to have in mind what you are specifically looking for in a Siberian. Are you looking for a nice companion that will live with you for the next decade and more? A winning show cat? A breeder?

Many people used to turn to their local pet shop when looking for a kitten or puppy. As a rule, this was not a good idea. Many pet shops "stock" only the popular breeds of pets that turn over quickly and make them a sizeable profit. The kittens were not born there, the staff don't know their parents, and hence have no idea of how this kitten may turn out as an adult in temperament, type, or health. Often, you can't see the other siblings and they certainly don't keep pictures. They can't tell you how many were in the litter, if the female had a good birthing record, or how they were handled early-on. Breeders, involved intimately in the care of their animals, will know all of these details and more.

Particularly since Covid, the internet is an ever-popular way to contact breeders worldwide. With the shut downs and isolation, it seems easy to just "order" one up. But you must be careful. Some breeders may not always be truthful. As a breeder, I always go with my gut feeling– if something isn't right, the person doesn't get my kitty. And conversely, if you are not comfortable with the breeder– even if they presumably have the perfect kitten for you, I would look elsewhere. Sadly, many, many sites seem to pop up overnight and are clearly scams. Don't get fooled, or lose your hard-earned money. Genuine breeders have a track record, and can be found on registry websites like CFA.org and TICA.org to name just two.

A healthy kitten should exhibit a clean coat, clear eyes, and a playful disposition. It is highly doubtful that you are able to visit the breeder's home right now. But you can

Zoom, Facetime or use other electronic social media means of being able to interact with the breeder. You might be able to see the rest of the litter, provided they haven't been sold and placed already.

The home should be clean, but certainly doesn't have to be show-room meticulous! Remember, they have to live there with their family too! The mother of the litter should be available to be seen, and possibly the father. Do the parents appear healthy, friendly and handle-able? Is the breeder able to answer your questions directly? Can you see a pedigree? What associations are the litter registered in? What vaccines can you expect this kitten to have had by the time you are ready to take it home? And never expect to take a kitten home before it is 8 weeks old. This is federal law.

Any person/pet dealer/breeder who knowingly rehomes a kitten or puppy under this age is violating this law. Especially with your slow-to-mature breeds such as the Siberian, 8 weeks is extremely young. Most reputable, concerned, caring breeders will not let a kitten go to its new home until after 12-weeks of age. Most of these questions and concerns can be directly addressed by looking at the breeder's contract. Again, a reputable breeder will have a contract, and just as you are scrutinizing them, they in turn will be interviewing you. Be forthright in your answers, because only then can the breeder do their job and make sure the temperament of the kitten is a match for the needs of your home. If you leave some critical piece of information out, and the kitten doesn't fit into your home – that's on you, not the breeder, and it's the kitten who suffers.

There are many schools of thought regarding vaccines. Schedules, ideas, and laws vary from state to state and veterinarian to veterinarian. The governing board for feline practice in the US is the American Association of Feline Practitioners and their website offers guidelines in these matters: www.catvets.org.

When purchasing your kitten, a written contract is always a good idea. It protects you as the buyer by assigning certain guidelines to the breeder, and it protects the breeder by assigning certain criteria and limitations to the buyer. Don't be put off by a breeder who seems a bit nosy– asking possibly for vet references, pet sitter references, your kitty knowledge or experience. This is to help them make sure that the life they may entrust to you will be cared for in a wonderful new permanent home. Conversely, don't be afraid to ask to see the contract and question parts you do not understand. If you find a contract is very long and complicated, it may be simply in "legalese", or it may be that this isn't the breeder for you. When in doubt – Ask.

Before bringing your new kitten home, there are several areas you need to cover. First, and to my way of thinking most importantly, an appropriate litter box and litter. Again, don't hesitate to ask the breeder which brand of litter they use and prefer. Changing litter on a kitten say from a clay-based to a clumping type is never a good idea. It can lead to the kitten choosing to potty somewhere *other* than the box. Also, make sure the box is in a semi-private area where the kitten can have easy access to it, with minimal disturbance. A high-traffic area can also cause any kitty to choose another, more private location, other than their litter box.

Many people give little thought to food bowls, but these

can have an impact on kitty. I recommend metal bowls as they can easily be cleaned or sanitized. They don't break when dropped or get chewed on, and are readily available in many styles, sizes, and varieties. Plastic is generally a bad idea as it pits and scars very easily making sanitation virtually impossible. While often shatter-proof, plastic bowls can chip or crack leaving sharp edges, possibly hurting kitty. Plastic can also harbor bacteria potentially causing feline acne.

Fresh water is also a consideration most people don't give much thought to. If bringing your kitty in from another region, water changes can be a major source of tummy upset and possibly even diarrhea. Using filtered water, such as from a pitcher filter or one that fits over the faucet itself are both inexpensive and easy solutions. Also, as kitty ages there often are varying degrees of mineral content that have the potential for medical problems, such as kidney damage or urinary blockage. Both are life-threatening illnesses, and possibly preventable with a simple filter for your water.

Food should be as close to what the breeder recommends as possible, at least for the first few weeks. Any sudden change in diet can result in upset tummies and diarrhea. Ideally the breeder will give you a sample of the actual diet. If this is not possible, be especially sure to get the name and variety, and what stores might carry it.

Once you get your new kitty home, be sure to have a special room set aside. One that is closed off from the rest of the house where there is a litter box, food and water but other pets or children do not have ready access.

Your new kitty will most likely be very confused and upset by this new move. It is much safer if kitty has a chance to acclimate slowly by getting used to the sounds and smells of your home over a period of a week or more. If it is an adult you are bringing home,  this transition can take weeks or even months, depending on circumstances. Patience is the key phrase. Go in as often as possible during this time and sit with the kitty, talk to the kitty, play with and pet your new kitty. After a period of time, you can let your new family member out by just opening the door. The room is a safe place that your kitty can, and will retreat to after some initial exploring. Remember, a stressed cat becomes a sick cat, so limiting stress is paramount.

Not Getting Taken

Sadly, in today's world this must be discussed, and at great length. Scams/scammers and thieves are just one of the pitfalls you need to look out for, especially in this digital age. Make sure the website you are accessing is legitimate. Make sure the cattery name they are using is in fact theirs, and registered with one of the registering bodies, such as CFA, TICA, ACFA to name the US domestic registries. That information can be found on the registries' websites, and you need to check each one individually. Make sure the breeder has not used other people's photos! That's a big one! Many legitimate breeders watermark their photos, and these thieves take them, putting them on their websites even with the other cattery name on them! You can always check out the digital registry at https://lookup.icann.org to see how old a website it. A good clue you are dealing with a scammer is that the website is a week old. Use good judgment and caution. Misspelled words and even wrong words (i.e. using "puppy" for "kitten") can be good indicators of a bad site. Also having a long list of "available" kittens and "buy it now" buttons are all indicators of potential trouble.

Another way of getting taken is by so-called-breeders who release their babies at 8 or 9 weeks of age. This is absolutely not condoned by any reputable breeder, and can and will bring about many psychological problems as well as potential health problems. Siberian babies need to stay with their family unit for at least a minimum of 12 weeks to develop proper social skills, to wean properly and to develop good litterbox habits. Weaning in cats is a lengthy process, not a "one-and-done". It affects their confidence, their social interaction skills, their personalities and more. A breeder who takes a baby away from its mother that young is permanently harming such a young kitten. Then there is the financial aspect of that. A breeder who responsibly raises their kittens, will ensure that they are well-socialized, handled, and given at least two if not three sets of upper respiratory vaccines prior to leaving.

Kittens should have been dewormed at least one time, and we advocate the early spay/neuter of all kittens not being specifically placed into a breeder's home. Feeding a kitten for the additional month of time, plus all the extra veterinary costs, now have been foisted onto the unsuspecting or uneducated buyer. Be a smart buyer and do your homework.

Siberians are a slow-to-develop breed, needing as long as 5 years to fully mature. Take your time and get the life-long companion not only that you deserve, but that the cat deserves.

CHAPTER 10

FUN CAT FACTS AND

A RUSSIAN FOLK TALE

S ome basic facts are true for all domestic cats whether they are a pedigreed Siberian or a common alley cat:

Fun Cat Facts

🐾 Pregnancy duration (gestation) is 63 days on average, ranging from 57 to 65.

🐾 Cats have 244 bones while people only have 204.

🐾 Cats have 30 muscles in their ears!

🐾 Normal healthy body temperature is 100° to 102.5° F.

🐾 Heart rate is an average of 240 beats per minute.

🐾 Cats are obligate carnivores. They do not need grain as we feed today. Their teeth are not designed to eat grain, even if we put it in those cute and colorful shapes.

* A cat does *not* always land on its feet. Use care around plant shelves, open windows, lofts, open stair cases and other high places your Siberian might find to explore.

A Russian Folk Tale of Interest

This is the translation of an old Russian folk tale I find interesting. It is of the mistaken identity and relationship between a fox and a cat. What makes this particular tale noticeable is the name given to the cat and where the character claims to hail from. (*Translated from the Russian by Tanya and D'Mitry Vasilev with our thanks and gratitude.)

"The Cat and The Fox"

There was a man. This man had a cat, but this cat was such a trickster, it was terrible! The man grew dead tired of him. He thought about it a good long time, then he took the cat, put him in a bag, and took him to the forest. Once there, he just left the cat to fend for himself if he could.

The cat wandered and wandered for a long time, and came upon a small izba [ed. Note- log house]. He climbed into the attic and curled up there. When he got hungry, he would go out in the forest and catch a few birds and a few mice, eat his full, and climb back into the attic, and he was happy!

Once the cat went out for a walk, and saw the fox

coming up. The fox saw the cat was very puzzled. "I've lived many years in the forest, and I've never seen such an animal!"

She bowed to the cat, and asked him, "Tell me, brave youth, who are you? How did you come into these parts, and what is your name?"

The cat puffed up his fur and said, "My name is Kotofei Ivanovich, I hail from the Siberian forests, and I have been sent here to be your governor!"

"Oh, Kotofei Ivanovich!" the fox said, "I did not know about you, I had no idea! Well, won't you come to my house."

The cat went to the fox's house. She took him to her den and began feeding him all sorts of game, and continued to ask him about himself.

"Kotofei Ivanovich, are you married or a bachelor?"

"A bachelor."

"So am I! Won't you marry me!" The cat agreed, and they feasted and made merry.

The following day the fox set out to find more food, and the cat stayed home. The fox spent all *morning hunting, and finally caught a duck. She was carrying it home when she encountered the wolf.*

"Stop, fox! Give me that duck!"

"Certainly not!"

"Then I'll take it from you!"

"And I'll tell Kotofei Ivanovich, he'll execute you!"

"And who is this Kotofei Ivanovich?"

"Haven't you heard? He was sent from the Siberian forests to be our governor! I used to be the fox maiden, but now I am the governor's wife!"

"No, I hadn't heard, Lizaveta Ivanovna. Could I take a look at him?"

"Oh, my Kotofei Ivanovich is so short-tempered: if someone displeases him, he'll eat him right away! You had better get a ram and bring it to him as a welcoming gift. But be careful, put the ram in an open place, and hide yourself so that the cat doesn't see you, or else, brother, woe will befall you!"

The wolf ran off to get a ram, and the fox went home. On her way, she met the bear.

"Stop, fox! Give me that duck!"

"Certainly not!"

"Then I'll take it from you!"

"And I'll tell Kotofei Ivanovich, he'll execute you!"

"And who is this Kotofei Ivanovich?"

"Haven't you heard? He was sent from the Siberian forests to be our governor! I used to be the fox maiden, but now I am the governor's wife!"

"No, I hadn't heard, Lizaveta Ivanovna. Could I take a look at him?"

"Oh, my Kotofei Ivanovich is so short-tempered: if someone displeases him, he'll eat him right away! You had better get a steer and to bring it to him as a welcoming gift. But be careful, put the steer in an open place, and hide yourself so that the cat doesn't see you, or else, brother, woe will befall you!"

The bear ran off to get a steer, and the fox went home.

The wolf brought a ram, skinned it, and stood there, thinking. Who should he see, but the bear arriving with a steer on his back.

"Good day, Mikhailo Ivanovich!"

"Good day, brother Levon! Have you seen the fox and her husband?"

"No, Mikhailo, I'm waiting for them myself."

"Why don't you go up to their door and call them," the bear said to the wolf.

"No, I won't go, Mikhailo Ivanovich. I'm not very nimble, you'd better go."

"No, I won't go, I'm shaggy and pigeon-toed, I certainly can't go!"

Suddenly, out of nowhere, a hare came running by. The wolf and the bear yelled at him! "Come right here, Cross-Eyes!"

The hare stopped dead in his tracks and flattened his ears.

"You're nimble and fast on your feet. Go run up to the fox's den and tell her that the bear Mikhailo Ivanovich and brother Levon Ivanovich have been ready for some time, and are waiting for you and your husband, Kotofei Ivanovich. They're bringing a ram and a steer as welcoming gifts."

The hare ran as fast as he could to the fox's den. Meanwhile, the bear and the wolf started thinking where they could hide.

The bear said: "I'll climb on the pine-tree." The

wolf answered: "How about me? I can't climb on trees! Hide me somewhere." The bear hid the wolf in the bushes, covered him up with dry leaves, and climbed up on the pine tree, up to the very top, and kept watch for Kotofei Ivanovich and his wife. Meanwhile, the hare arrived at the fox's den.

"The bear Mikhailo Ivanovich and the wolf Levon Ivanovich sent me to tell you that they have been waiting for some time to see you and your husband. They want to offer a ram and a steer as welcoming gifts.

"Go on, Cross-Eyes, we'll be right there."

So the cat and the fox went out. The bear saw them and said to the wolf, "What kind of a governor is this Kotofei Ivanovich, he's so small!"

The cat jumped on the steer, puffed up his fur, and began tearing at the meat with his teeth and his paws, purring all the time and sounding angry. "Meow, meow", but the bear and the wolf heard "more, more".

The bear said to the wolf, "He may be small, but what a glutton! We couldn't eat this meat between the four of us, and he says it's not enough for him alone! He may yet get to us!"

The wolf wanted to take a good look at Kotofei Ivanovich, but he couldn't see him through the leaves. So he started to push the leaves away carefully. The cat heard the leaves rustling, and thought it was a mouse, and jumped at the wolf! He landed right on his nose, and caught him with his claws!

The wolf was so frightened that he leapt away and ran off as fast as he could. The cat was frightened, too, so he climbed up the tree where the bear was hiding.

"That's it," the bear thought, "he saw me!" There was no time to climb down. The bear just fell down, hurt his bottom, jumped up, and ran away as fast as he could.

The fox called after them, "Run, run, or he might skin you yet!"

And from then on, all the animals feared the cat. The cat and the fox, meanwhile, had enough meat for the whole winter, and they lived happily ever after, and still live there to this day.

What makes this tale so interesting is first the cat's name being "Kotofei". *Kot* is Russian for "cat" and *kotofei* is a respective derivative of *kot* to make it sound like a name. Something similar to this would be, rather than saying Tim, we would say "Timothy". And remember "Kotofei" was and is the name of a cat club in Russia.

Second is where fox tells wolf that cat is from the Siberian Forest. Just how old this tale is, is unknown, but one author has it as over 300 years; yet most believe it to be 19th Century in origin.

QUICK GLOSSARY

ACFA – American Cat Fanciers Association. Founded in 1955 promotes the welfare and education of all domesticated pedigreed and non-pedigreed cats.

CFA – Cat Fanciers Association. The world's largest registry of pedigreed cats founded in 1906.

Pedigreed – Is the known recording of a line of ancestors. A continuous history of precedents, often used as proof of desired qualities.
  • **Note** - pedigreed does not mean "purebred". Most breeds of cats, (most notably Scottish Folds, Bombays, Selkirk Rex, Minuets, and Ragamuffins to name a few), are derived from breeding a "purebred" member of its breed to a pedigreed member of another breed (or in some cases even a domestic short/longhair). This can expand the gene pool keeping the working population healthier but can also introduce new disease traits and genetic anomalies as well.

Purebred – an animal that is bred from recognized members of its own designation over many generations without the admixture of other types or strains.

TICA – The International Cat Association. Founded in 1979 from a handful of former ACFA member, is now one of the foremost genetic registries in the world

BIBLIOGRAPHY / SOURCES / REFERENCES /

Bibliography

Books:

Ashford, Grace and Pond, Alison E. *Rex, Abyssinian and Turkish Cats.*
London: John Gifford Ltd, 1972.
ISBN: 978-0707100838

Edwards, Alan and McHattie, Grace. *The Big Book of Cats, Illustrated Guide to More Than 60 of the World's Favorite Breeds.*
Philadelphia: Courage Books, 1999
ISBN: 978-0762405978

Jude, A. C. *Cat Genetics.*
Jersey City: T.F.H Publications, 1967.
LCCN: 55012060

Morris, Desmond. *Cat Breeds of the World.*
New York: Viking, 1999
ISBN 978-0670886395

Weir, Harrison. *Our Cats and All About Them.*
Tunbridge Wells: R. Clements and Co., 1889.
LCCN: 2002554760

Wright, Michael and Walters, Sally. *The Book of the Cat.*
New York: Summit Books, 1980.
ISBN: 978-0671416249

Magazines:

The writings of Elizabeth Terrell of Starpoint Cattery:

1. *Cat Fancy Magazine,* October 1988.

2. *Cat World International,* Jan/Feb 1991.

3. *Cat World International,* Nov/Dec 1991.

Sources

A huge note of thanks to Read Country Books and specifically Ben Read for allowing me generous usage of material from their production of *Our Cats and All About Them* by author Harrison Weir original publication date 1889, reprint copyright 2006. Please visit them on the web at: www.readcountrybooks.com .

Photographs:

A special thank you to Richard Katris of Chanan Photography for his permission to use his work. www.chanan.com

(All copyrights are retained by the photographer, Richard Katris of Chanan Photography, all rights reserved. Used only with exclusive permission.)

Photographs appear on pages: 13, 50, 86.

Again, a huge note of thanks for allowing me to use his photos in this work:

George Lewis, Feline Photographer. He can be reached at: abykatz@cableone.net .

(All copyrights are retained by the photographer, George Lewis, all rights reserved. Used only with exclusive permission.) Photographs appear on pages: 6, 7, 45, 69, 84.

Colorpoint Siberian Kittens Photo Courtesy of Croshka Siberians, Page 58.

Colorpoint Siberian Cats "Hercules" and "Ali", Photos Courtesy of Prekrasne Siberians, Pages 58, 59.

Scanned Documents and Drawings:

1883 American Cat Show Cat Show Catalogue and *Entry No 163*, Courtesy of the Harrison Weir Collection, Page 19.

Public Domain Engraving Picture originally from *Rural Sports* published in 1813; reprint is from *Our Cats and All About Them* by Harrison Weir (listed previously under "Books"). Page 18.

Pallas Cat Drawing

Pallas, Peter Simon. *Pallas's Travels Through the Southern Provinces of the Russian Empire in the Years 1793 and 1794.*

London: Sherwood, Neely, and Jones, 1812.

Public Domain file from Smithsonian Libraries and Archives:

https://www.flickr.com/photos/smithsonianlibraries/44 75952585/ Page 54.

Original pen and ink drawings by Alice Wright- All rights reserved, and contracted specially for this publication. Pages 63, 66, 67, 68.

References

Cat Clubs:

American Cat Fanciers Association (ACFA)
http://acfacat.com/

The Cat Fanciers' Association, Inc. (CFA)
https://cfa.org/

The International Cat Association (TICA)
https://tica.org/

DNA Screening Services:

A short list of recognized and respected US-Based DNA screening services:

Optimal Selection
https://optimal-selection.com/

Cat Scan
https://www.mycatscan.com/

UC Davis Veterinary Genetics Laboratory (Featured Tests for Cats)
https://vgl.ucdavis.edu/tests?field_species_target_id=216

Recommended Reading:

Cluster, Cassie. *Potty Training for REAL Cats: Cat Toilet Training for Humans and Felines.*
Phoenix: Picky Press, 2021.
ISBN: 9781643949963   LLCN: 20211931954
(Features 2 Kender Siberians!)

ABOUT THE AUTHOR

Trainer, instructor, breeder and author Alice Wright has been involved with purebred cats all her life. Her professional involvement started in the mid-1980s when she began breeding and exhibiting Maine Coons, Siamese, Oriental Shorthairs, Colorpoint Shorthairs, and a Japanese Bobtail. In 1992, she began her love affair with the Siberian Cat, and has dedicated herself to the breed's preservation and improvement. Her cattery, Kender, is one of the first names in the breed, and has produced many of the top winning and producing Siberians in the US.

Alice has over a decade of experience as a veterinary assistant and pet nutritionist. She has been actively involved in dog training and handling. Alice Wright has several published articles that have received international interest. She currently resides in Arizona with her husband, two children, German Shepherd dogs, and Siberian Cats.

Other Books by Alice E. Wright That You Might Enjoy...

The global cat food market in 2021 reached a value exceeding $33 BILLION USD, and promises only to grow. Your cat's health, and perhaps very life, may depend on the choices you make. Why are pet foods made the way they are? Who makes them, who is responsible for them? This book gives you the knowledge to make the best, most well-informed choice for your family.

You want the best for your feline companion. Offering raw food to your feline is what she is hardwired for, what her body craves and what makes her thrive. *The Raw Facts of Feline Feeding* by Alice E. Wright gives you all of the important essentials that you need in order to make sure your cat has the healthy diet they were meant to have. Find out how to make your cat's food from scratch, or learn what types of food are available to fit your unique situation and your budget. Learn from an expert in the field.

Give your Journaling experience the fun and whimsy it needs by sharing your writing with all of these Siberian Forest Cats and Kittens in *The Siberian Cat Journal* by Alice E. Wright.
Each lined page contains a beautiful Siberian cat or kitten living their best cat days!

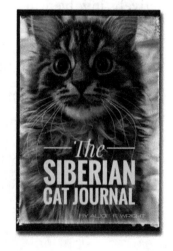